Reflections for the Effective Capital Campaigner

A book of the Effective Philanthropy and Fund Raising series.

Reflections for the Effective Capital Campaigner

Quotes, axioms and observations to help you expand our important institutions

Jim Norvell

Writers Club Press
San Jose New York Lincoln Shanghai

Reflections for the Effective Capital Campaigner
Quotes, axioms and observations
to help you expand our important institutions

Writers Club Press
an imprint of iUniverse, Inc.

For information address:
iUniverse, Inc.
5220 S. 16th St., Suite 200
Lincoln, NE 68512
www.iuniverse.com

Artistic license was exercised with the quotes borrowed from an illustrious array of thoughtful people. Insertion of their observations in juxtaposition to my own was based on their unique similarity, often taken out of context. Those who are still around to do so are free to do the same with mine.

ISBN: 0-595-20876-2

Printed in the United States of America

For all of my mentors, DMA and Brakeley colleagues.

To My Campaign Brethren

During my fund-raising career, I have had the privilege to be involved in over 75 major fund-raising campaigns. The key lesson from that body of experience is that money is really a secondary concern in a capital campaign. Other, human, elements are much more central–none more than the troika of driving force leadership. That leadership is composed of influential volunteers, inspirational nonprofit managers and savvy, goal-driven fund-raising professionals. If any of the three is weak, the campaign will not realize its potential.

There is no way to overestimate the importance of any of these leadership sources. It has always been *de rigueur* to place the campaign chair and other top volunteer leadership at the pinnacle but, truthfully, I have never witnessed a campaign success where the chief executive was weak or the fund-raising plan was inappropriate. If there is ever a time for a full-inclusion partnership of the three, it is during a capital campaign.

Back to the original premise–capital campaigns had better be about something a lot more important than money. Organizations mobilizing their constituents and communities for substantial increases in funding must be able to demonstrate that the investment will have an extraordinary yield. The size of the goal has no bearing on the impact of these transformational experiences. Raising $1 million for a women's shelter should be as exciting and rewarding for the participants as raising $2 billion for Harvard University. The importance of a capital campaign is not relative; it is absolute.

The capital campaign is a statement of will, but it had better be a statement of potential. I have witnessed a universal phenomenon; a successful capital campaign has far greater ramifications than the organization's leadership ever foresees. The successful campaign creates a new organization, not just a bigger one—an organization that recognizes its past only as a developmental phase of what it is to become. The bar is raised, but the confidence level jumps even while pressed to keep pace with ever-escalating expectations.

Capital campaigns are for the achievers, not the mere hopeful. They are successfully conducted on both the record and the opportunity. When you are involved in a capital campaign, do everything in your power to be worthy of the organization's reputation and the promise of its future. Have fun, too – it's easier that way.

Jim Norvell

History will be kind to me for I intend to write it.

Winston Churchill

Quotes, axioms and observations to help you expand our important institutions

This book was compiled as a resource for those engaged in capital campaigns. It contains some of the key guidelines I have found to be useful in managing campaigns. It also provides quotations that may be used in various pieces of campaign literature to motivate volunteers and staff. Finally, I wrote it because I like quotes and have found that many of you share that enjoyment.

The most influential traits are those that exhibit sensitivity to others.

Quick sensitiveness is inseparable from a ready understanding.

Joseph Addison

Personal attributes generate more influence than authority.

I learned that a great leader is a man who has the ability to get other people to do what they don't want to do and like it.

Harry S. Truman

Enthusiasm and commitment should not be underestimated, especially of very wealthy people.

No one would remember the Good Samaritan if he had only good intentions. He had money as well.

Margaret Thatcher

No one solicits more effectively than a social equal of the prospect.

The pressure of social influence about us is enormous, and no single arm can resist it.

Felix Alder

The more impersonal the solicitation the less likely significant support.

I have known people to stop and buy an apple on the corner and then walk away as if they have solved the whole unemployment problem.

Heywood Broun

Donor prospects respond to example, peer challenge and incentive.

It is not fair to ask of others what you are not willing to do yourself.

Eleanor Roosevelt

The practical expression of power is leadership, but the possession of power does not insure leadership.

Power? The only power I've got is nuclear —and I can't use that.

Lyndon Baines Johnson

Style is an important element of leadership.

Every man of action has a strong dose of egoism, pride, hardness, and cunning. But all those things will be regarded as high qualities if he can make them the means to achieve great ends.

Charles DeGaulle

A leader is a symbol as well as a participant.

I was not the lion, but it fell to me to give the lion's roar.

Winston Churchill

Building shared vision is the leader's primary role.

*The only limit to our realization of
tomorrow will be our doubts of today.*

Franklin D. Roosevelt

Leaders inspire by communicating an exciting organizational future.

Our chief want in life is somebody who will make us do what we can.

Ralph Waldo Emerson

The more powerful the leadership, the higher the motivation.

*Winning isn't the only thing but wanting
to win is.*

Vince Lombardi

The board members' is to insure their organization operates above all applicable laws.

In the search for ways to maintain our values and pursue them in an orderly way, we must look beyond the resources of the law.

Dean Acheson

Someone has to show the way for others.

Do it big or stay in bed.

Opera promoter Larry Kelly

Leadership can make or break a campaign and its participants.

A team should be an extension of the coach's personality. My teams were arrogant and obnoxious.

Al McGuire

Strong boards are fund-raising boards.

A few highly endowed men will rescue the world for centuries to come.

John Henry Newman

A strong board is an accident without a good nominating committee.

Quality represents the wise choice of many alternatives.

Will A. Foster

If the board chair will not lead, who will follow?

I have always had a dread of becoming a passenger in life.

Princess Margrethe of Denmark

Board members whose only financial experience is balancing their own checkbook have a difficult time making strategic decisions.

Experience is in the fingers and head. The heart is inexperienced.

Henry David Thoreau

Organizational structure must allow for control.

Discipline is the soul of an army. It makes small numbers formidable, procures success to the weak, and esteem to all.

George Washington

Commitment to shared values shapes the organizational culture.

If you don't have a shared value system, you don't have an inner source of security.

Stephen R. Covey

The ideal nonprofit is professionally managed and volunteer led.

The test of a first-rate intelligence is the ability to hold two opposed ideas in the mind at the same time, and still retain the ability to function.

F. Scott Fitzgerald

A weak fund-raising board is a deficiency that no paid fundraiser can overcome.

Life is something like a trumpet. If you don't put anything in, you won't get anything out.

W. C. Handy

No one solicits as effectively as a committed volunteer, only the chief staff officer is a close second.

Ya gotta do what ya gotta do.

Sylvester Stallone (as Rocky Balboa in "Rocky IV")

No paid employee carries the credibility of a committed volunteer.

You give little when you give of your possessions. It is when you give of yourself that you truly gain.

Kahlil Gibran

Everyone has a power base built on ability, knowledge, relationships and authority.

If money is your hope for independence you will never have it. The only real security that a man can have in this world is a reserve of knowledge, experience and ability.

Henry Ford

Good fundraisers possess expert power.

But where's the man who counsel can bestow, still pleas'd to teach, and yet not proud to know?

Alexander Pope

Everyone possesses power to some degree and uses it both well and poorly.

Money hasn't really been an issue for me for quite a while. I just do what I feel like—that's all there is to do.

Jack Nicholson

Power must be used by a nonprofit for tactical advantage.

There is no meaning to life except the meaning that man gives his life by the unfolding of his powers.

Erich Fromm

With change comes opportunity, without comes threat.

If it ain't broke, break it.

Dave Brubaker

The ultimate objective of strategy is to position the organization to control a market segment.

Positioning is thinking in reverse. Instead of starting with yourself, you start with the mind of the prospect.

Al Ries and Jack Trout

"Owning the market" starts with knowing the competition's strengths and your weaknesses.

A horse never runs so fast as when he has other horses to catch up and outpace.

Ovid

Strategy capitalizes on established strengths.

*I never came to the party thinking
I could dance.*

Ali MacGraw

Philanthropic strategy differentiates a nonprofit organization as uniquely worthy.

What is worth in anything
But so much money as 'twill bring?

Samuel Butler

Plans are driven by implementation strategy.

Thoughts are energy. And you can make your world or break your world by thinking.

Susan Taylor

Strategy builds a values bridge between the organization and its constituency.

Man is the creature that cannot emerge from himself, that knows his fellows only in himself; when he asserts the contrary, he is lying.

Marcel Proust

A shared power strategy offers all of the collateral benefits that nonprofit managers seek.

Power must always feel the check of power.

Louis Brandeis

There are different levels of strategy.

Keep the villain chasing the girl.

Randall Miller

Effective strategy recognizes that implementation takes longer than the sum of individual activities.

Everything takes longer than it should,
with the possible exception of sex.

Jim McGinn

Specific goals and the means to reach them define strategy.

Speed isn't that important in stealing bases. It's the first two steps that count.

White Herzog

Strategic planning is a vision-refinement process.

People can die of mere imagination.

Geoffrey Chaucer

A David vs. Goliath strategy may be inspiring, but few nonprofits need to make quantum leaps.

With audacity one can undertake anything, but not do everything.

Napoleon I

A wish list can only be realized through planning.

There is really nothing to say—except why.
But, since why is difficult to handle, one
must take refuge in how.

Toni Morrison

All organizations require planning and each is improved by a commitment to it.

The most formidable obstacles lie at the beginning. Once these have been surmounted, the path is comparatively smooth.

Winston Spencer Churchill

Private agendas are informal plans.

Egotism is the anesthetic that dulls the pain of stupidity.

Frank Leahy

Limitations are often overcome by looking at the organization from a different perspective.

If the waitress has dirty ankles, the chili should be good.

Al McGuire

Good planning is both inclusive and liberating.

Make no little plans; they have no magic to stir men's blood.

Daniel Hudson Burnham

Planning is more important than plans, planners more important than planning.

In the construction of a country it is not the practical workers but the idealists and the planners that are difficult to find.

Sun Yat-Sen

The budget is the enabling mechanism of a plan.

I don't like money actually, but it quiets the nerves.

Joe Louis

Plans replace the continuity lost by undertaking change.

I reject get-it-done, make-it-happen thinking. I want to slow things down so I can understand.

Jerry Brown

Plans establish boundaries and create focus.

We must ask where we are and whither we tender.

Abraham Lincoln

A plan without measurable objectives is useless.

If wishes were horses, beggars might ride.

English Proverb

Plans should free managers to exercise all their capabilities, not to restrict them.

If everyone is thinking alike then somebody isn't thinking.

Gen. George S. Patton, Jr.

Sustained performance is rarely achieved without sustained planning.

One of life's most painful moments comes when we must admit that we didn't do our homework, that we are not prepared.

Merlin Olsen

Basic human fears, inertia and inexperience hobble the planning process.

Paralyze resistance with persistence.

Woody Hayes

Plans should be guides for managers, with built-in latitude for change.

Ideals are like stars; you will not succeed in touching them with your hands. But like the seafaring man on the desert of waters, you choose them as your guides, and following them you will reach your destiny.

Carl Schurz

Planning is doomed without a powerful advocate to overcome inhibited thinking.

Deliberation is the work of many men.
Action, of only one.

Charles DeGaulle

A board member should lead planning.

The buck stops here.

Harry Truman

Capital campaigns require a much higher level of organizational commitment than annual campaigns.

If you don't invest very much, then defeat doesn't hurt very much and winning is not very exciting.

Dick Vermeil

The capital campaign, more than any other form of fund raising, is an act of faith.

Faith embraces many truths
which seem to contradict each other.

Blaise Pascal

The feasibility study is a pro forma
campaign commitment, but not
a campaign launch.

I respect faith, but doubt is what gets you education.

Wilson Mizner

A major campaign is no time to look for shortcuts and lowest cost bids.

Don't look for speed in a cheap horse, be content if it neighs.

African proverb

A capital campaign must be the chief executive's top priority.

Our duty is to be useful, not according to our desires but according to our powers.

Henri Frédéric Amiel

A capital campaign tests the commitment of the organization's most able donors and leadership.

Don't be afraid to take a big step if one is indicated. You can't cross a chasm in two small jumps.

David Lloyd George

Capital campaigns require a deep knowledge of organizational behavior.

This is going to be complicated.

Kelly McGillis to Tom Cruise in "Top Gun"

Capital campaigns must be executed with a sense of urgency.

The best is the enemy of the good…a good plan violently executed now is better than a perfect plan next week.

Gen. George S. Patton, Jr.

A capital campaign changes the organization more than any other type of fund raising.

When our first parents were driven out of Paradise, Adam is believed to have remarked to Eve: "My dear, we live in an age of transition."

William Inge

A capital campaign goal should stretch the organization to the limit of its capability without exceeding it.

Accept the challenges, so that you may feel the exhilaration of victory.

General George S. Patton, Jr.

A capital campaign shifts the balance of power within an organization.

There is no stronger test of a man's real character than power and authority, exciting as they do every passion and discovering every latent vice.

Plutarch

A capital campaign is most effectively conducted by the same leadership responsible for the strategic planning.

In dreams begin responsibility.

William Butler Yeats

Feasibility is not a dirty word, because the cardinal sin of fund raising is failure to reach an announced goal.

Wishes are not goals, wills are goals.

Jefferey Hodges

The feasibility interview is a powerful pre-selling tool.

Conversation has a charm about it,
an insinuating and insidious something
that elicits secrets from us
just like love or liquor.

Seneca

Feasibility studies determine the strength of organizational links to constituent values.

*Awareness of our own strength
makes us humble.*

Paul Cézanne

Discovering the leverageable equities of an organization is the first step in successful capital campaigns.

Differences challenge assumptions.

Anne Wilson Schaef

A good campaign plan is both detailed and flexible.

*I always preferred a running offense,
but I was smart enough to put in one
long incomplete pass per quarter
for the alumni.*

Duffy Daugherty

No nonprofit should initiate a feasibility study if it is not prepared to act swiftly on its recommendations.

Nothing is more difficult, and therefore more precious, than to be able to decide.

Napoleon I

The capital campaign has to start with board gifts.

Everybody wants to help, but nobody wants to be first.

Pearl Bailey

At least 10% of the goal should come from the board.

Few things are harder to put up with than the annoyance of a good example.

Mark Twain

A successful capital campaign is the hardest thing a volunteer will ever love doing.

If it wasn't hard, everybody would do it. It's the hard that makes it good.

Eddie Dolan (Tom Hanks), "A League of Their Own"

About the Author

James R. (Jim) Norvell

Jim is a second-generation fundraiser who began his career immediately after graduating from Southern Illinois University–Edwardsville. He served in annual fund positions at Monticello College, the Foundation for Independent Colleges of Pennsylvania and Washington University before joining G. A. Brakeley & Co., Inc., Los Angeles, as a capital fundraiser. He left Brakeley to form his own capital campaign consulting firm, Development Management Associates, Inc. (DMA) and to earn his MBA at UCLA. Over fifteen years, he and partner Bob Zuer expanded DMA to $2 million in annual billings, serving clients throughout the Western United States, Great Britain and Australia.

0-595-20876-2